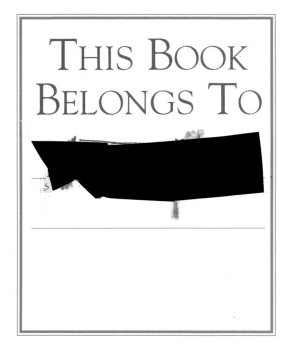

THIS BOOK BELONGS TO

The Old Testament

MOST OF THE EVENTS OF THE Old
Testament take place in a small area to the east of
the Mediterranean Sea. From ancient times
people have lived and travelled along a strip of
land known as the "fertile crescent", which
stretches from Egypt, through Canaan and
Mesopotamia to Babylonia.
There was enough water in this
area to enable them to grow
crops and graze animals.
Canaan, the "promised land",
where the Israelites flourished, is
only about 240km (150 miles)
from north to south. It contains
many different types of scenery,
including plains and river
valleys suitable for farming,
lakes, hills and rocky desert.

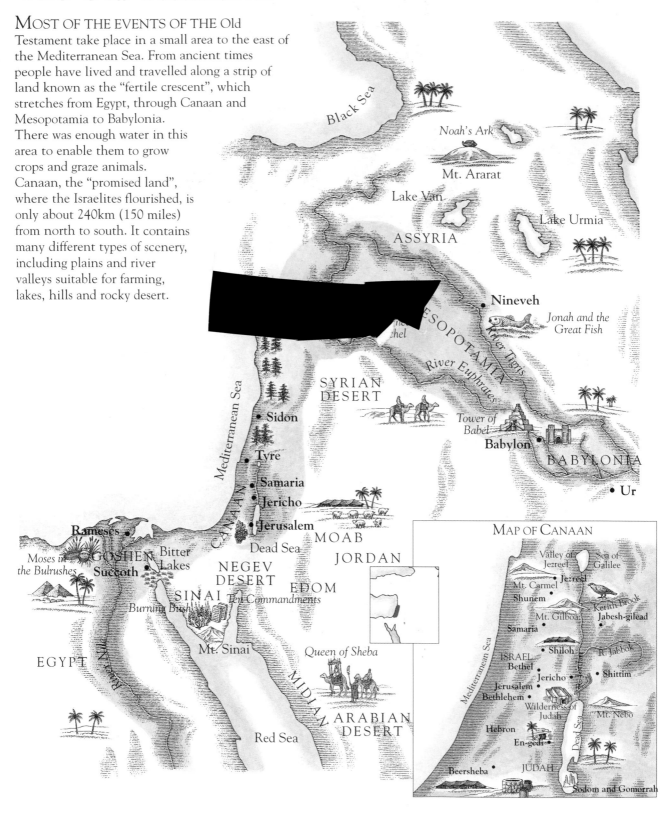

Black Sea

Noah's Ark

Mt. Ararat

Lake Van

Lake Urmia

ASSYRIA

Nineveh

Jonah and the Great Fish

River Tigris

MESOPOTAMIA

River Euphrates

SYRIAN DESERT

Sidon

Tower of Babel

Babylon

BABYLONIA

Tyre

Samaria

Jericho

Ur

Jerusalem

MOAB

Dead Sea

Rameses

Moses in the Bulrushes

GOSHEN

Bitter Lakes

JORDAN

Succoth

NEGEV DESERT

EDOM

SINAI Ten Commandments

Burning Bush

Mt. Sinai

Queen of Sheba

EGYPT

MIDIAN

ARABIAN DESERT

Red Sea

MAP OF CANAAN

Valley of Jezreel

Sea of Galilee

Jezreel

Mt. Carmel

Shunem

Kerith Brook

Mt. Gilboa

Jabesh-gilead

Samaria

R. Jabbok

Shiloh

Shittim

ISRAEL

Bethel

Jericho

Jerusalem

Bethlehem

Wilderness of Judah

Mt. Nebo

Hebron

En-gedi

Dead Sea

Beersheba

JUDAH

Sodom and Gomorrah

Mediterranean Sea

Noah's Ark

• And other Bible stories •

Retold *by* Selina Hastings

DORLING KINDERSLEY
London • New York • Stuttgart

A DORLING KINDERSLEY BOOK

Art Editor   Shirley Gwillym
Project Editor   Marie Greenwood
Senior Editor   Emma Johnson
Designer   Sarah Cowley
Additional design by
Heather Blackham, Muffy Dodson
Production   Ruth Cobb, Marguerite Fenn
Managing Editor   Susan Peach
Managing Art Editor   Jacquie Gulliver

Introduction and section openers written by
Geoffrey Marshall-Taylor

CONSULTANTS
Educational Consultant
Geoffrey Marshall-Taylor,
Executive Producer, BBC Education,
Responsible for religious radio programmes
for schools

Historical Consultant
Jonathan Tubb,
Western Asiatic Department
British Museum, London

Religious Consultants
Mary Evans
London Bible College

Jenny Nemko
Jewish writer and broadcaster for the BBC

First published in Great Britain in 1996
by Dorling Kindersley Limited
9 Henrietta Street, London WC2E 8PS

The Children's Illustrated Bible
Copyright © 1994 Dorling Kindersley Limited, London
Text copyright © 1994 Selina Hastings
The right of Selina Hastings to be identified as the Author
of this Work has been asserted by her in accordance with
the Copyright Designs and Patents Act 1988.

A CIP catalogue record for this book is available from the
British Library.

ISBN 07513-5485-6
Reproduced by Colourscan, Singapore
Printed and bound in Spain by Artes Graficas
Toledo S.A.   DL:TO-328-1996

Extracts from the Authorised Version of the Bible (The
King James Bible), the rights of which are vested in the
Crown, are reproduced by permission of the Crown's
Patentee, Cambridge University Press.

CONTENTS

Introduction to the Bible

MEDIEVAL BIBLE
A decorative page from an 8th-century Bible in the Royal Library in Stockholm.

THE BIBLE IS A collection of books written by different people over a period of more than 1,000 years and dating from about 1450BC. It is divided into two main parts, the Old Testament and the New Testament.

The Old Testament books are the Scriptures, or sacred writings, of the Jewish people. They give an account of the people of ancient Israel over many centuries. By contrast, the New Testament, which consists of writings about Jesus and his first followers, covers a period of about 60 or 70 years. Both the Old and New Testaments make up the Christian Bible.

There are 66 books in the Bible. It is often said that it is more like a library because there are so many kinds of writing in it. For example, there are books containing laws, history, poetry, wise sayings or proverbs, diaries, and letters.

The Old Testament
The 39 books of the Old Testament have guided the Jewish people throughout their history. These are the Scriptures which Jesus read. For Jews, the most important part is the Torah – the first five books of the Bible. The word "Torah" means "teaching". The five books are Genesis, Exodus, Leviticus, Numbers, and Deuteronomy. Christians call this the "Pentateuch", a Greek word meaning "five books".

Each Sabbath Jewish congregations listen to a part of the Torah being read from scrolls in the synagogue. It takes a year of weekly readings to go from the beginning to the end. On the day when the last part of the Torah is reached and Genesis chapter one is due to be read again, there is a celebration called *Simchat Torah*, the "rejoicing of the law". A procession dances around the synagogue carrying the Torah scrolls high in thanksgiving.

In Christian services passages from the Old Testament are often read. The stories are considered important by Christians because of what can be learned from them about God, about others, and about themselves.

The Five Books of Moses
The Torah is special to Jews because its books contain God's words given through Moses to the Hebrew people, their ancestors. The Torah is sometimes referred to as "The Five Books of Moses" because of this. Its stories, songs, prayers, and laws teach about God and what he promises to his people and expects from them.

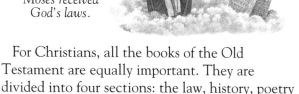

On Mount Sinai, Moses received God's laws.

For Christians, all the books of the Old Testament are equally important. They are divided into four sections: the law, history, poetry and wisdom writings, and the prophets.

At first the words of the earliest books of the Old Testament were passed on by one generation repeating them to the next. Eventually they were written down in the Hebrew language on parchment, which is made from animal skin. Each word was copied carefully by a scribe, as it is today.

A rabbi, or teacher, studies the words of the Torah.

A Jewish boy becomes Bar-Mitvah at the age of 13.

The Torah is studied by young Jews from an early age. When a Jewish boy reaches the age of 13 he becomes *Bar-Mitzvah*, which means "a son of the commandment". He is now a Jewish adult and, on the Sabbath after his birthday, he can read from the Torah in the synagogue. A Jewish girl becomes *Bat-Mitzvah* (daughter of the commandment) at the age of 12. Some synagogues mark the occasion with a special ceremony.

The Dead Sea Scrolls
In 1947 a shepherd boy came across some ancient scrolls in caves near the Dead Sea: they were fragments of all the books of the Old Testament, except for Esther, and had probably been written out at the time of Jesus. It is thought that they came from the monastery at Qumran and were hidden in the caves by a group of Jews called the Essenes. The discovery showed how accurately scribes had copied these special words down the centuries.

Psalm 119 verse 105 explains why the Old Testament is so important to Jews and Christians. The writer says to God, "Your word is a lamp to my feet and a light to my path".

DISCOVERY
The Dead Sea Scrolls, stored in pottery jars, were found in caves at Qumran (below). Some of the fragments date back to the 2nd century BC.

The Creation

I N THE BEGINNING God created heaven and earth. Water lay deep over the surface of the earth and the darkness was absolute. God said, "Let there be light." And there was light. God divided the light, which he called day, from the darkness, which was night. And so ended the first day and night of creation.

Next God said, "Let there be sky over the waters," and he called the sky heaven; and this was on the second day.

On the third day dry land rose up through the waters, and God called the land earth, and the waters sea. At once grasses took root on the earth and every kind of plant; buds opened, seeds sprouted and trees grew heavy with fruit.

On the fourth day God said, "There must be lights in the sky to divide night from day and to mark the seasons." For this he created two lights, the greater, which he called

On the first day God creates light

On the second day God creates sky

On the third day God creates land, sea and every kind of plant

the sun, to shine over the day, and the smaller, the moon, to shine at night. Around the moon he set the stars.

On the fifth day God created all the creatures of the sea and sky. Birds flew through the air, while in the watery depths great fish swam silently. On the sixth day he made all the animals, from the wild beasts of desert and jungle to cattle grazing in the fields.

And God said: "I shall make man to rule over them." And so from the soil itself God created mankind, both male and female in his own likeness. And that was on the morning and the evening of the sixth day.

On the seventh day God rested, for his work was done, and he saw that all was well with the world.

On the fourth day God creates the sun, the moon and the stars

On the fifth day God creates the creatures of the sea and sky

On the sixth day God creates animals and mankind

The Garden of Eden

SERPENT
Serpents or snakes, like the Egyptian cobra above, were thought by many people to represent evil or Satan. In the book of Genesis, Satan opposes God and tries to upset his plans.

CHERUBIM
Cherubim were often represented as winged sphinxes, or human-headed lions, as in this Assyrian ivory carving. In the book of Genesis, cherubim act as God's attendants. They guard the Tree of Life, which is the symbol of eternal life.

I N THE EAST, in Eden, God made a Garden in which grew every tree and plant, and at the very centre stood the Tree of Life and the Tree of Knowledge. God put Man into the Garden, telling him he might eat any fruit he wished except from the Tree of Knowledge: for if he were to eat that, he would die.

God brought to the Man, Adam, all the animals, so that he might name them. He then sent Adam into a deep sleep, and while he slept, took one of his ribs and out of it made Woman, so that Adam should have a wife. Both Adam and Eve, his wife, walked naked and happy in the Garden, and had no need of clothes.

Now the Serpent, the most devious of all living creatures, questioned Eve, asking her if she could eat any fruit she pleased. "Yes," she said. "Any fruit except that from the Tree of Knowledge. If we eat that, we die."

"But you will not die," said the Serpent. "Instead you will discover the difference between Good and Evil, and so be equal with God."

The Woman gazed at the Tree, and was tempted by the juicy fruit that would make her wise. She picked one and ate it; gave one to her husband, and he ate it. As they looked at each other, they

Adam and Eve are happy in the Garden of Eden

*Eve picks a fruit from
the Tree of Knowledge
and gives it to Adam*

became aware of their nakedness. They quickly gathered some fig-leaves which they sewed together to cover themselves.

In the cool of the evening they heard the voice of God as he walked in the Garden, and they hid so he should not see them. God called to Adam, "Adam, where are you?"

Adam said, "I heard your voice, and I was afraid so I hid."

"If you are afraid then I know you must have eaten from the Tree whose fruit I told you not to eat."

"It was the Woman who gave me the fruit."

And Eve said, "It was the Serpent, that tempted and deceived me."

Then God cursed the Serpent, and banished him from the Garden. He gave clothes to Adam and Eve, saying, "Now that you know both Good and Evil, you must leave Eden. You cannot stay for fear you might eat also from the Tree of Life, and if you did that you would live for ever." And God drove them out of the Garden, and into the world. At the east of Eden he stationed cherubim and placed a flaming sword to guard the entrance to the Garden and to the Tree of Life.

*God drives Adam and Eve out of
the Garden into the world*

Noah's Ark

CYPRESS TREES
Cypress trees are found throughout the Bible lands. The wood is light, but strong and long-lasting. It was an ideal choice of timber for a boat as large as the ark.

A S THE YEARS PASSED, the descendants of Adam grew in number and spread to the four corners of the earth. But as they grew in number, so they grew in wickedness; and God, seeing violence and corruption everywhere, decided to destroy all the people and animals that he had created.

There was, however, one man whom the Lord loved, a good man who led an honest and hard-working life. His name was Noah, and God chose to save him, and to save also Noah's wife, and his three sons, Shem, Ham and Japheth, and their wives.

"The world has grown wicked," he told Noah, "and I intend to destroy every living thing that I have made. But you, Noah, you and your family shall be saved.

Noah and his sons build the ark

Noah

"BUT WITH THEE WILL I ESTABLISH MY COVENANT; AND THOU SHALT COME INTO THE ARK, THOU, AND THY SONS, AND THY WIFE, AND THY SONS' WIVES WITH THEE."
GENESIS 6:18

"I shall cause a flood to rise over the land, and you must build an ark out of cypress wood which will float on the waters; it must be roofed with reeds and coated inside and out with tar. It must measure three hundred cubits long, fifty cubits wide and thirty cubits high. It shall have three storeys, with a door and a window in the side. In it you must make room for yourself and your family, and two – one male, one female – of every kind of creature, every kind of beast, reptile and bird. And you must fill it with enough food for them and for yourselves. For it will rain for forty days and forty

THERE WENT IN TWO AND TWO UNTO NOAH INTO THE ARK, THE MALE AND THE FEMALE, AS GOD HAD COMMANDED NOAH.
GENESIS 7:9

The animals enter the ark, two by two

nights, and life on earth will be extinct."

Noah did exactly as God had told him: he and his sons built the ark, making it watertight and stocking it with plenty of food of every variety for man and beast. When everything was ready, they led all the animals into the ark. Then they themselves went inside and shut fast the door.

The skies darkened and it began to rain.

BOAT BUILDING
Noah and his sons would have built the ark by hand. The planks of wood were coated with tar to make the boat watertight. This traditional method of boat building is still practised in parts of the Middle East today.

The Flood

THE RAIN CONTINUED for forty days and nights. The flood waters rose, lifting the ark up with them until it was floating as high as the hills. Finally even the mountain ranges were submerged, and everything that was alive perished: there was no living thing left on earth.

But God had not forgotten Noah, and all who were with him on the ark. After a time the rains stopped. The days went by, and then a great wind blew up; and after the wind a calm, and slowly the waters began to go down. Eventually the ark came to rest on a mountain peak in Ararat.

THE DELUGE
This engraving by Gustave Doré captures the plight of people caught in the flood.

Every living thing perishes in the flood

AND THE WATERS PREVAILED, AND WERE INCREASED GREATLY UPON THE EARTH; AND THE ARK WENT UPON THE FACE OF THE WATERS.
GENESIS 7:18

Time passed, and Noah wanted to find out if the waters had subsided. Opening a window, he released into the air a raven to see if the bird would find anywhere to land. But the raven flew far and wide in every direction and saw nothing but water.

Next Noah released from the ark a dove; but she, too, flew in every direction without finding anywhere to land, for the waters still covered the earth. She returned to the ark, and Noah tenderly took her in. After seven days he again sent out the dove, and this time she came back in the evening with the leaf of an olive tree in her beak.

Noah knew by this that the waters were receding, and after waiting another seven days he sent out the dove once more. This time she did not return. Opening a window in the ark, Noah looked out and saw that the ground was dry.

God then spoke to Noah. "Now you must leave the ark, you and your sons and their wives, and all the creatures you have with you. The world is for you and your children to govern, and the beasts on land and birds of the air and fish in the sea shall provide your food."

Then Noah built an altar in thanksgiving and made an offering on it to God. God was pleased with the sacrifice and blessed Noah and his family, telling them that they and their descendants would cover the earth.

As he spoke his blessing, a rainbow appeared in the sky. "This rainbow," he said, "is a sign that never again will the world be destroyed by flood; and in times to come when I cloud the sky with rain, afterwards you will see a rainbow, and you will remember my promise, a promise made to you and to every living creature in the world."

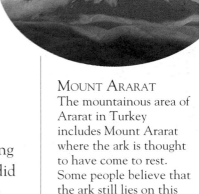

MOUNT ARARAT
The mountainous area of Ararat in Turkey includes Mount Ararat where the ark is thought to have come to rest. Some people believe that the ark still lies on this peak and expeditions have been sent to find its remains.

AND THE DOVE CAME IN TO NOAH IN THE EVENING; AND, LO, IN HER MOUTH WAS AN OLIVE LEAF.
GENESIS 8:11

The flood waters rise for forty days and nights

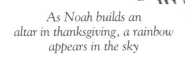

As Noah builds an altar in thanksgiving, a rainbow appears in the sky

The Tower of Babel

THE DESCENDANTS OF NOAH, having wandered for many years in the lands of the east, settled eventually on a wide plain in Shinar. Centuries had passed since the flood, and now there was a great number of them, all speaking the same language. They decided between them to build a city out of brick, with a tower so tall its top would touch the clouds. This would give them a home, they thought, from which

BABYLON
Babel is traditionally thought to be the ancient walled city of Babylon, the capital of the empire of Babylonia. The earlier, biblical, name for Babylonia was Shinar.

The people of Babel build a tower out of brick that reaches to the sky

tar for mortar

mud bricks

nobody could drive them out. More importantly, it would make them envied throughout the world.

And so they began to build, baking the bricks hard and using tar for mortar.

The Lord looked at the city which was taking shape, at the streets and the houses and the tower already rising up into the sky, and he said to himself, "These people are growing vain. Soon there will be no limit to what they will want. I will confuse their speech, change the very words in their mouths, so that nobody will understand what is said."

And so it was: soon everyone found that the words spoken by one person meant nothing to their neighbour.

This caused complete confusion. The building of the city, which was now called Babel because of the babble of voices within it, came to a stop. The people left the plain of Shinar and were scattered all over the world.

And in every part of the world from that time on both men and women spoke in different languages.

ZIGGURAT
The tower of Babel may have been a ziggurat, or temple tower. Ziggurats have been found in Babylon and Ur. The pyramid-like buildings have outside staircases that lead to a temple at the top. Here, people believed they could be closer to the gods.

As the people talk to one another, they find their speech is confused

MUD BRICKS
The tower of Babel may have been built out of mud bricks. To make the bricks, mud and straw are mixed together, shaped in wooden moulds, then left to dry in the sun. This method of building is still used in parts of the Middle East today.

Abram's Journey

ABRAM WAS A RICH MAN who was born in Ur in Mesopotamia. Now elderly, he had settled with his wife Sarai in Haran. It was a sadness for both of them that they had had no children. One day God spoke to Abram. "You must leave this place, Abram, and take your wife and your relations and servants and everything you possess, and move to the land of Canaan. Once there you will have my blessing, your name will be great and your people will become a great nation."

ABRAM'S JOURNEY
The map shows the most likely route taken by Abram and Lot when they journeyed from Ur to Haran and on to Canaan. Lot finally settled in Sodom.

Lot's people

Lot and Abram decide to part and Lot's people move to the plain of Jordan

Lot   *Abram*

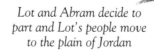

TREASURES FROM UR
This gold helmet and dagger with its decorative case, or sheath, were discovered in Ur, a powerful city state and the birthplace of Abram and Lot.

So Abram, with his wife Sarai and his nephew Lot, with his servants, his gold and silver, his donkeys and camels, sheep and cattle, travelled south to the land of Canaan.

But at the first place they settled there was not enough fertile land. Abram's shepherds began to fight Lot's shepherds for the best place to graze their flocks. Abram said to Lot, "Let us not quarrel. The whole country lies before us. You go to the east, and I to the west, and there will be plenty for everyone."

So Abram and his people settled in Canaan, while Lot looked to the east and saw the plain of Jordan. It was as lush and green as a well-watered garden. And there Lot agreed to go, he and his people settling in Sodom, one of the cities of the plain, whose inhabitants were known to be great sinners.

The Lord spoke again to Abram. "Look around you: all this land will belong to you and to your many descendants."

"But how can I have descendants?" said Abram, "I am an old man and I have no children."

"You will have a son," God told him. "And your son will have children, and his children's children will be as many in number as there are stars in the sky."

THE LORD MADE A COVENANT WITH ABRAM SAYING, "UNTO THY SEED HAVE I GIVEN THIS LAND, FROM THE RIVER OF EGYPT UNTO THE GREAT RIVER, THE RIVER EUPHRATES."
GENESIS 15:18

Abram's people settle in the land of Canaan

Sarai

Then God told Abram to make a sacrifice: to take a cow, a she-goat and a ram; to kill the animals, cut them in half and lay them side by side; to kill also a turtledove and a young pigeon.

This Abram did, dividing the animals in two, and leaving the birds whole. Later in the day he beat off the birds of prey which greedily swooped down upon the carcasses. As the sun set he fell into a deep sleep, and while he slept he was seized with a terrible fear. But then he heard the voice of God speaking to him. He promised Abram that all would be well, and that he and his descendants would live in prosperity and die in peace.

Night fell; and suddenly there came out of the darkness smoke and flames and a burning torch which passed over Abram's sacrifice.

DESERT WANDERINGS
Abram and his family led a nomadic life. They travelled from place to place, looking for grazing land and water for their animals. They carried all their possessions on camels, and lived in tents. The Bedouin people live a similar life in the desert today.

Abram, Sarai and Hagar

TENT DWELLERS
Desert dwellers today, such as these modern Bedouin, live much like Abram's family did. Because they constantly travel with their flocks to new grazing land, all of their possessions must be light, and easy to roll up. Waterproof tents woven out of coarse goat hair are homes well suited to this way of living.

SARAI WAS GROWING OLD and still she had no children. She went to her husband, Abram, and told him that he should have a child by Hagar, her servant. "Look on Hagar," she said, "as though she were your wife."

This Abram did, but once Hagar realized she was going to have a baby, she began to put on airs and act rudely towards her mistress. "Hagar now looks down on me and insults me," Sarai complained to Abram.

"You must deal with her as you think right," Abram replied.

Upon this Sarai began to treat her servant so harshly that Hagar ran away into the desert.

An angel found Hagar beside a spring in the wilderness, where she was weeping.

"What are you doing here?" he asked her.

"I am running away from my cruel mistress."

"You must return and behave well towards her. You are soon to give birth to

Hagar is expecting a child by Abram and begins to put on airs in front of Sarai

20

a son whose name shall be Ishmael, and his descendants will be numbered in millions." So Hagar returned and shortly afterwards gave birth to a boy.

Abram was then eighty-six years old. He looked at his son and gave him the name Ishmael, which means "God hears".

When Abram was ninety-nine, God appeared to him and said, "You shall be the father of many nations, and to mark this you must change your name to Abraham. I will keep my promise to you, and Canaan shall belong to you and your descendants for ever; and I will be their God. Among your people every male must be circumcised now, and every male child of future generations. This will be a sign that you will keep your promise to me. From now on your wife must be called Sarah, and she will be the mother of your son."

Abraham laughed to himself at the idea that a man of ninety-nine and a woman of ninety should have a child. But God said, "Sarah will indeed have a son, and you shall call him Isaac, and he will be the father of princes. It will be with Isaac that my promise shall be continued, a covenant to be kept with all his descendants throughout all their generations.

"As for Ishmael, I will bless him and always look after him. He will lead a long and prosperous life, and will have many children. He will be a great power in the land, even though it is his brother, Isaac, whom I have chosen as the father of my people."

Hagar runs into the wilderness and weeps, as Sarai has treated her harshly

MOTHER AND CHILD
This Bedouin woman is holding her little child close to her. The Israelites considered children to be a gift from God. To be barren and unable to have a child, as Sarai was for many years, would have caused much heartache. Children spent most of their early years with their mother.

Hagar   Abram

Hagar returns home and gives birth to a boy, and Abram calls him Ishmael

Abraham and Sarah make the three strangers welcome

Abraham

Sarah

The three strangers tell Abraham and Sarah that they will have a son

milk

unleavened bread

calf meat

curds

DESERT MEAL
Sarah prepared a meal of bread, which may have been unleavened (made without yeast); milk, from a goat or sheep; curds, made from soured milk; and calf meat. The welcome given to the three strangers reflects the hospitality of desert nomads.

Time passed, and God appeared to Abraham near the trees of Mamre in the heat of the day.

Abraham was sitting at the entrance to his tent when he looked up and saw three strangers standing before him. At once, he came out to greet them. "My Lord," Abraham said, bowing low. "If I have found favour with you, do not pass me by. Come, sit under this tree so you may wash your feet and rest, then we will bring you food, for we are your servants." Abraham then hurried back into the tent, giving orders to Sarah to bake bread, and for a tender young calf to be roasted. He stood by the three strangers under the tree while they ate.

"Where is your wife?" they asked.

"She is in the tent."

"Soon she will bear you a son."

Now Sarah was listening to this and she laughed at the idea that such an old woman should bear a child. But the Lord heard her and rebuked her.

"Do you think there is anything too difficult for God to do?" he said to her.

Sodom and Gomorrah

OD TOLD ABRAHAM that he intended to destroy the cities of Sodom and Gomorrah, because their inhabitants were guilty of terrible crimes.

"If you find even ten good people," Abraham implored him, "will you have mercy and save these cities from destruction?"

"If I find ten good people," said the Lord, "I will not destroy them."

Two angels left for Sodom. They arrived there in the evening, where they were met at the city gates by Abraham's nephew, Lot. He welcomed them to his house, and spread before them a feast which he had prepared with his own hands.

No sooner had they finished eating than they heard the noise of a large crowd gathering. It was the men of Sodom: they were demanding that Lot hand over to them his two guests for their own pleasure. Lot was full of anger and went out to speak to the crowd. "I would rather give you my daughters, to do with as you please," he said. "But these two you must not harm for they are guests under my roof."

THE LORD SAID, "BECAUSE THE CRY OF SODOM AND GOMORRAH IS GREAT, AND BECAUSE THEIR SIN IS VERY GRIEVOUS, I WILL GO DOWN."
GENESIS **18:20-21**

Lot goes out to speak to the crowd

Lot

A large crowd gathers threateningly outside Lot's home

The crowd was in a frenzy and took no notice, the men only shouted louder and tried to force their way in. Suddenly Lot felt the angels' hands on his shoulders: they pulled him inside and shut the door. Then they struck the crowd with blindness, so that the men could no longer see where they were.

The two angels said to Lot, "Are there any other members of your family here? You must go to them and tell them to leave at once or they will die when the city is destroyed." Lot hurried to his daughters' husbands and warned them of what was about to happen, but they would not listen and refused to move. Then the angels told Lot that he himself must leave. "Take your wife and both your daughters, and go quickly, for we must destroy this place and all its wickedness."

By now dawn was breaking, and the angels urged Lot to be gone.

CITIES OF THE PLAIN
The cities of Sodom and Gomorrah probably lay in what is now the southern end of the Dead Sea. This area was once dry land which was very fertile. It is thought that an earthquake caused the Dead Sea to spread and cover the towns.

God rains down fire and brimstone on Sodom and Gomorrah

When they saw him hesitate, they took him by the hand and led him through the deserted streets and out beyond the city walls.

"Run as fast as you can, and make straight for the mountains. And on no account look behind you."

Lot's wife turns to look behind her and is transformed into a pillar of salt

Lot and his two daughters flee to the city of Zoar

"I cannot go so far," said Lot. "The mountains are too distant. Let me stay instead in the city of Zoar. Let me live there, and let it not be destroyed." And to this the angels agreed.

By the time the sun had risen Lot had reached Zoar. Then the Lord God rained down fire and burning stone on Sodom and Gomorrah, so that they and their people and the surrounding plain and everything that grew and moved upon it were utterly destroyed. Feeling the heat and hearing the noise, Lot's wife turned to look behind her. Instantly she was transformed into a pillar of salt.

The next morning Abraham rose early, and going to the place where he had talked with the Lord, he looked towards Sodom and Gomorrah. Instead of those two great cities of the plain he saw nothing but thick black smoke like the smoke from a giant furnace.

PILLARS OF SALT
Because of the large amount of salt in the Dead Sea, nothing can live there – hence its name. There are clusters of salt to be found in the water, which serve as a reminder of the terrible fate of Lot's wife.

The Sacrifice of Isaac

NEGEV DESERT
Abraham and Isaac set off from their home in Beersheba. They journeyed through the Negev Desert, in southern Canaan, for three days until they reached Moriah.

GOD SPOKE TO ABRAHAM, in order to test his faith. "With your beloved son Isaac you must go to the land of Moriah, to a certain mountain which I will show you. There, instead of a goat or lamb, you must sacrifice your son on the fire."

The next morning, obedient to God's will, Abraham saddled a donkey, and set off for Moriah, taking Isaac and two servants with him. When they got to the mountains, Abraham stopped to cut some wood, giving it to his son to carry. He himself took a sharp knife and a flaming torch with which to light the fire. "You must stay here with the donkey," he told the two men. "We are going up the mountain to pray and make an offering to God."

"Father," said Isaac as they started on their way. "We have the wood for a fire, but where is the lamb to be sacrificed?"

"God will provide," answered Abraham.

When they reached the place chosen by God, Abraham built an altar on which he piled the wood; then, tying Isaac's arms tightly to his sides, he placed the boy on top of the pile. Abraham lifted the knife high above his head, preparing to plunge it into Isaac's breast. But at that moment he heard the voice of the angel of the Lord.

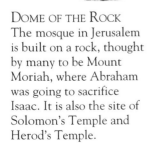

DOME OF THE ROCK
The mosque in Jerusalem is built on a rock, thought by many to be Mount Moriah, where Abraham was going to sacrifice Isaac. It is also the site of Solomon's Temple and Herod's Temple.

The two servants wait with the donkey

Abraham and Isaac go up the mountain to offer a sacrifice to God

"Abraham, Abraham, do not hurt your son. You have proved your perfect love of God by your willingness to sacrifice even your child."

The angel of the Lord tells Abraham not to hurt Isaac

RAMS IN THE THICKET
Abraham saw a ram, or male sheep, caught in a bush and sacrificed it instead of his son. The ram's horns may have become entangled as it tried to feed from the branches of the bush.

A ram caught in a thicket is sacrificed instead of Isaac

Looking round, Abraham saw a ram caught by the horns in the tangled branches of a bush. He untied Isaac, and seizing hold of the ram, put the animal on the altar in place of his son.

The angel spoke again. "Because you have done this for the love of God, you will be blessed, and your son, and your son's sons will be blessed; and they shall be as many in number as the stars in the sky."

Then Abraham and Isaac came down from the mountain, and with the two servants returned to Beersheba.

"IN BLESSING I WILL BLESS THEE, AND IN MULTIPLYING I WILL MULTIPLY THY SEED AS THE STARS OF THE HEAVEN, AND AS THE SAND WHICH IS UPON THE SEA SHORE."
GENESIS 22:17

Isaac and Rebekah

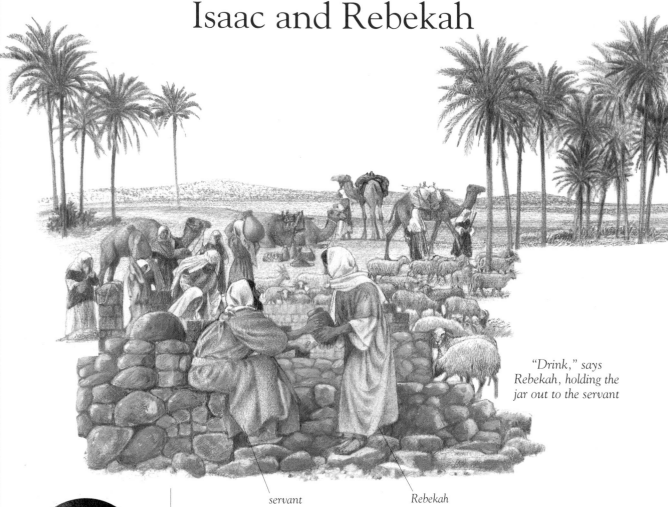

"Drink," says Rebekah, holding the jar out to the servant

servant   Rebekah

WATER CARRIER
Women like Rebekah often went to fetch water from a community well or cistern. These usually lay outside the city gates.

SARAH WAS DEAD, and Abraham knew he himself had not long to live. He sent for his most trusted servant. "My people are settled in Canaan, but I do not want my son to marry a Canaanite. You must go to the land of my birth, and from there bring back a wife for Isaac."

And so the servant set off for the city of Nahor in Mesopotamia, taking with him a train of ten camels laden with rich gifts. He arrived outside the city walls in the evening when the women were gathering to draw water at the well. As he watched them he prayed to God for a sign: "Let her whom I ask for water be the wife for Isaac."

Almost before he had finished his prayer, a young girl carrying a water jar came to take her turn at the well. Her name was Rebekah, and she was very beautiful. The servant went up to her. "Will you let me drink from your jar?" he asked.

"Drink," she said, holding the jar out to him. "And now I will fetch water for your camels as well."

The servant was overjoyed at her kindness.

CAMEL
Abraham's large herd of camels was a sign of his family's wealth. The camel was used as a working animal. It was capable of carrying up to 180 kg (400 lb) and could travel across the desert at about 13-16 km (8-10 miles) an hour.

Covering her face with a veil, Rebekah goes to meet Isaac

Isaac

From a saddlebag he took a heavy gold nose-ring and two bracelets of solid gold and gave them to her. "Where do you live?" he asked. "May I stay at your father's house?"

"You are welcome," replied Rebekah. Then she hurried home to tell her family. Her brother Laban welcomed the stranger, soon recognizing that it was God's will that Rebekah should return with him to Canaan.

Abraham's servant, having sent a prayer of thanks to God, made gifts to Rebekah of gold and silver jewellery and beautiful embroidered cloth. The next morning Rebekah said goodbye to her family, then set off with her nurse and servants for her new home.

Isaac was praying in the fields at twilight when he saw the camel caravan approaching through the dusk.

Covering her face with a veil, Rebekah dismounted. The servant described everything that had happened, and Isaac took Rebekah by the hand and led her to his tent.

Soon afterwards they were married, and Isaac loved his wife and was comforted by her for the death of his mother, Sarah.

NOSE-RING
The nose-ring given to Rebekah may have looked like the one this Bedouin woman is wearing. Mesopotamian women often wore jewellery, including rings, necklaces, and bracelets.

Esau and Jacob

IBEX
Esau would have hunted game such as the ibex, a type of wild goat, whose meat was highly prized. Ibexes are still found in rocky areas of the Middle East today.

AFTER MANY YEARS OF CHILDLESSNESS Rebekah gave birth to twin boys. The elder, who was covered from head to toe with thick red hair, they named Esau. The younger, they called Jacob. Esau, whom Isaac loved best, grew up a strong and adventurous hunter, while Jacob, his mother's favourite, preferred staying at home.

One day Jacob was cooking some lentil stew when his brother came in faint with hunger. "Quick, I'm famished! Give me some of that!" Esau demanded.

"I will," Jacob replied, "if you in return give up your rights as the first-born son to me."

Esau laughed. "What use to me are rights when what I want is a good meal!"

"Then give me your word." And Esau gave his word, and so exchanged his birthright for a plateful of stew and some bread.

Isaac, old and blind and near to death, asked Esau to shoot a deer and prepare the dish of venison he so loved. "I want to taste it one last time so that I may bless you before I die," he told him.

Esau, whom Isaac loves best, is a hunter

Jacob, Rebekah's favourite, prefers staying at home

Esau exchanges his birthright for a plateful of stew

Rebekah overheard these words and determined that Jacob, not Esau, should receive his father's blessing. "I will cook the dish," she said, "and you must take it to your father in Esau's place. Go now and fetch me two young goats."

"But he will know I am not Esau!" said Jacob. "Esau is covered in hair, and my skin is smooth. He will know that I am deceiving him, and will put a curse on me!"

"Do as I say, and all will be well." And Rebekah dressed Jacob in his brother's clothes and covered his hands and shoulders with goatskin. She gave him some bread and a bowl of stew made from goat's meat. Then she sent him to his father.

"Who are you?" Isaac asked, puzzled. "Come near me so that I may feel you. These are Esau's hands but you speak with the voice of Jacob. Are you really my eldest son?"

"I am," Jacob lied.

So Isaac was deceived. Believing that it was Esau who was with him, he ate the food that had been brought to him. He blessed Jacob and promised that he should have everything due to the first born. "May you be happy and prosperous, and may good fortune come to all who wish you well."

LENTIL STEW
Esau sold his birthright to Jacob in exchange for a "mess of pottage", or red lentil stew, which he scooped up with thin unleavened bread. This was a typical meal in Old Testament times.

Rebekah discovers that Isaac is to give Esau his blessing

Rebekah helps Jacob to disguise himself as Esau

Isaac blesses Jacob instead of Esau, while Rebekah looks on

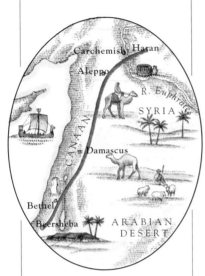

JACOB'S JOURNEY
Jacob set off from
Beersheba in southern
Canaan. He stopped at
Bethel, where God
appeared to him in a
dream. From there he may
have followed the route of
the trade caravans and
passed through major
cities, such as Damascus,
before reaching Haran.

Scarcely had Jacob left his father's tent than Esau arrived home from the hunt. Expertly he prepared the dish of venison and took it to Isaac. "Here is your favourite dish, father," he said.

"Who are you?" asked the old man.

"I am Esau, your eldest son."

"Then who is it who has just now been with me, and to whom I have given my blessing?" Isaac asked, his voice trembling.

When Esau heard his father's words, he cried out bitterly. He realized the trick that had been played, and he begged his father to bless him and give him his rights.

"I will bless you," said Isaac, "but I cannot give you what I have already promised to your brother." As Isaac knew that in the blessing was the word of God, and it could not be altered.

Esau was filled with hatred for Jacob. He knew that Isaac would soon be dead, so he planned to kill Jacob as soon as the period of mourning for his father's death had passed. But Rebekah heard of his plot and was able to warn Jacob. "Your brother is planning to kill you," she told him. "Go at once to my brother Laban in Haran, and stay there until Esau's anger cools. I will let you know when it is safe to return." So Jacob left Beersheba and set out for Haran.

Esau cries out when he realizes that Isaac has blessed Jacob

Rebekah tells Jacob to leave for Haran, to escape his brother's anger

Jacob's Ladder

O N HIS WAY TO STAY with Laban, Jacob stopped for the night. He picked up a large, smooth stone to use as a pillow and lay down to sleep.

He dreamt he saw a stairway reaching up to heaven, with angels moving up and down it. At the top of the stairway was God. "I am the God of Abraham and of your father Isaac," said the Lord to Jacob. "And I will give the land on which you lie to you and your descendants."

When Jacob woke early the next morning, he was struck with wonder. "This is a holy place, for God himself was here." He took the stone which he had used as a pillow, and having stood it upright, poured oil over it. Then he named the place "Bethel", meaning the house of God.

Jacob dreams of a stairway reaching like a ladder to heaven

AND HE DREAMED, AND BEHOLD A LADDER SET UP ON THE EARTH, AND THE TOP OF IT REACHED TO HEAVEN: AND BEHOLD THE ANGELS OF GOD ASCENDING AND DESCENDING ON IT.
GENESIS 28:12

Jacob falls asleep, using a stone as a pillow

Jacob and Rachel

Jacob

Rachel

Jacob watches as Rachel approaches the well

SHEPHERDESS
Rachel was a shepherdess.
She would have tended
her flock with care,
protecting it from harm.

J ACOB CONTINUED on his journey from Bethel.
Eventually he came near to Haran, in northern
Mesopotamia. He saw a field in the middle of which
was a well covered by a large, heavy stone. Round the well
lay several flocks of sheep, being tended to by shepherds.
Every day when it was time for the sheep to drink, the
shepherds would lift off the stone and draw water for the sheep
from the well. They would then replace the stone back over the
mouth of the well.

Jacob greeted the shepherds. "Can you tell me the name of this
place?" he asked.

"You are in Haran," they told him.

"Do you know Laban?"

"We know him well," they replied. "His daughter, Rachel, will be coming soon to draw water for their sheep."

Jacob sat down and waited, and then he saw Rachel approaching, driving before her a flock of sheep. Jacob thought she was very beautiful.

As she drew near, Jacob lifted the stone from the top of the well and helped her water her father's sheep. "I am Jacob, the son of Isaac. My mother is Rebekah, your father's sister," he told Rachel. Then he embraced and kissed her.

Rachel was delighted to see her cousin. She ran at once to tell her father the news.

Laban, too, was filled with joy, and hurried to meet his nephew.

JACOB'S KISS
On first meeting Rachel, Jacob kisses her. This painting by William Dyce tenderly captures the moment.

On hearing from Rachel that Jacob is here, Laban comes out to greet his nephew

Rachel and Leah wait to welcome Jacob

Throwing his arms around Jacob, he told him how glad he was that he had come. "You are welcome to my house," he said. "You, my sister's son, must come and stay with me."

They went back to his home where both Rachel and her elder sister, Leah, were waiting to welcome Jacob to their father's house.

So Jacob, having told his uncle all that had happened between himself and Esau, stayed with Laban for a month. During that time he worked hard, doing willingly whatever Laban asked him.

HEBREW BEAUTY
Rachel would have been young, with a natural beauty like this girl.

Jacob's Return

*Jacob and his family
journey home to Canaan*

stranger

Jacob

A stranger wrestles with Jacob

JABBOK RIVER
Jacob sent his family
across the Jabbok River,
so that he could spend
some time alone. The
fast-flowing Jabbok feeds
into the River Jordan.

FTER THE BIRTH OF JOSEPH, Jacob decided it was time to leave
Laban, who was becoming jealous of his skills as a shepherd
and his growing wealth. He sent a message to Esau to say he
was on his way home and that he hoped Esau would look favourably
on him. And then, taking with him his wives and children, all his
servants, his herds and flocks, he started out for Canaan. Almost at

once word came that Esau was coming to meet him with a force of four hundred men.

"I fear from this that he means to attack," said Jacob, and prayed to God to save him. He divided his own company into two parts, so that if Esau did attack at least half would escape. Then he chose a large number of cattle, camels and donkeys to give to his brother.

That evening Jacob sent all the men, women and children, together with his possessions, across the Jabbok River so that he might have some time alone.

Suddenly, and from nowhere, a stranger appeared and began to wrestle with him.

ESAU MEETS JACOB
The dramatic reunion of the two brothers is realistically captured by Gustave Doré in this 19th century engraving.

Jacob   Esau

Jacob and Esau are reunited

All night they fought in silence.

At dawn the stranger said, "It is now morning, and I must leave. Tell me, what is your name?"

" My name is Jacob."

"You shall not be called Jacob any longer, but Israel." And with that the stranger was gone. As the sun rose and light returned to the fields, Jacob realised that he had come face to face with God.

He had hardly caught up with his people when they saw a cloud of dust on the road, signalling the approach of Esau and his four hundred men. Jacob hurried forward, then bowed down before his brother. Esau threw his arms around him and kissed him, and they both wept. "Welcome, brother," Esau said. "You and yours are welcome home."

JACOB BOWED HIMSELF TO THE GROUND SEVEN TIMES, UNTIL HE CAME NEAR TO HIS BROTHER. ESAU RAN TO MEET HIM, AND EMBRACED HIM, AND FELL ON HIS NECK, AND KISSED HIM: AND THEY WEPT.
GENESIS 33:3-4

Joseph's Dreams

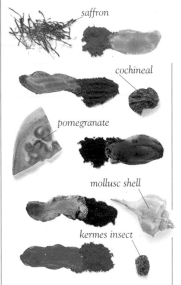

saffron

cochineal

pomegranate

mollusc shell

kermes insect

NATURAL DYES
Joseph's special coat
could have been dyed
with colours similar to
those shown above.
Orange came from the
saffron flower, pink from
the cochineal insect, blue
from the rind of a
pomegranate, purple from
the mollusc shell, and red
from the kermes insect.

JACOB LIVED IN CANAAN with his twelve sons. Of all his sons, he loved Joseph the most, as his mother was his beloved wife Rachel. He made Joseph a beautiful coat woven in all the brilliant colours of the rainbow. Jacob's other sons were jealous of Joseph because he was so favoured, and when they saw him in his coat of many colours they hated him. One night Joseph had a dream, and when he had told his brothers his dream, they hated him even more.

"I dreamt," he said, "that we were in the fields at harvest, tying up sheaves of corn. My sheaf of corn stood upright, while your sheaves bowed down to it."

Soon afterwards Joseph had another dream.

"I dreamt," he said, "that the sun and moon in the sky and eleven stars were all bowing down to me."

When the brothers heard his words they were furious. A few days later they took their flocks to graze in fields some distance away. Jacob sent Joseph to see that all was well. The brothers had a clear view

Joseph tells his brothers his dreams

Jacob gives Joseph a beautiful coat

of the road and saw Joseph approaching in his multicoloured coat. "Now is our chance – we could kill him and throw him into this pit. We can say that a wild animal attacked him."

But Reuben, who had a kind heart, spoke out. "Don't let us kill him: we don't want his blood on our hands. Much better just to throw him into the pit and leave him to his fate." And to this the brothers agreed – not knowing that secretly Reuben was planning to return later, rescue Joseph and take him home.

When Joseph reached them, his brothers attacked him at once, ripping off his coat and throwing him into the pit. They left him there without food or water. Then they sat down to eat.

At twilight a group of Ishmaelites came by. They were on their way to Egypt with camels loaded with spices, balm and myrrh. Judah suggested that they sell Joseph as a slave to the travellers. Then they would be rid of the brother they hated without having to kill him.

So Joseph was sold for twenty pieces of silver. And the Ishmaelites took him with them into Egypt.

Meanwhile the brothers killed a young kid and dipped Joseph's coat in its blood. Their father was filled with horror when they showed it to him. "This is Joseph's coat! My beloved son must have been killed by some wild beast!" Jacob tore his clothes in grief and wept, and no one was able to comfort him.

balm
cinnamon
fennel seeds
black peppercorns
myrrh oil
myrrh resin

ISHMAELITE GOODS
The Ishmaelite traders carried goods such as these from Arabia to Egypt. Cinnamon was used as a spice and a perfume, balm and fennel were used in medicine, myrrh resin and oil for anointing and embalming bodies.

A group of Ishmaelite traders are on their way to Egypt

The brothers throw Joseph into the pit

The brothers sell Joseph to the Ishmaelites

Joseph's coat

Joseph the Slave

WHEN THE ISHMAELITES ARRIVED IN EGYPT they sold Joseph to one of Pharaoh's officers, to Potiphar, captain of the guard. Joseph worked hard for Potiphar, who was so impressed by his skills that he made him head of his household.

Now Joseph was a handsome young man, and before long he

The Ishmaelites sell Joseph to Potiphar

Joseph

Potiphar

Potiphar's wife tries to seduce Joseph

WOMEN IN EGYPT
This Egyptian wall painting shows an official being offered food by his wife. Egyptian women like Potiphar's wife were powerful and could own and manage property.

caught the eye of Potiphar's wife. She tried very hard to seduce him, but Joseph resisted her. "Your husband trusts me," he said. "You cannot ask me to betray him." Potiphar's wife did not care for her husband or for Joseph's objections. Day after day she lay in wait, teasing and tempting him. And still he refused her. Then one day in desperation she cornered Joseph and caught hold of him by the sleeve of his coat. But Joseph was too quick for her, and he made his escape leaving her with nothing but an empty garment in her hands.

Then Potiphar's wife called all the servants. "Look what this Hebrew tried to do!" she said, holding up Joseph's coat. "He forced his way into my room, and when I cried out, he fled, leaving behind his coat."

When her husband came home, he was told the same false story. Potiphar, enraged, immediately had Joseph thrown into prison. Fortunately, however, the jailer took a liking to the young man, and put him in charge of all the other prisoners.

It so happened that in the prison with Joseph were Pharaoh's cupbearer and the royal baker. One night each of them had a dream, which in the morning they asked Joseph to explain. "In my dream," said the cupbearer, "I saw a vine with three branches, bearing ripe grapes. I squeezed the juice from these grapes into a cup, which I gave Pharaoh to drink."

"Your dream," said Joseph, "means that in three days Pharaoh will pardon you."

WALL PAINTING
The houses of officials such as Potiphar would have been decorated with brightly coloured wall paintings like this detail of a hunting scene. Raw materials, such as carbon for black and copper for green, were used as paints.

Potiphar and his wife have Joseph arrested

Joseph is led away to prison

cupbearer *Joseph* *baker*

Joseph explains the baker's and cupbearer's dreams

CUPBEARER
This limestone relief shows a cupbearer serving an Egyptian princess. The Pharaoh's cupbearer was a high-ranking official who held an important position of trust. His main duty was to taste food and drink before serving, to check for poison.

"I," said the baker, "dreamt that I had three baskets of bread for Pharaoh stacked on my head, and a flock of birds flew down and ate every crumb."

Joseph looked grave. "I am sorry to say that your dream means that in three days Pharaoh will have you hanged."

And it happened just as Joseph said: within three days the cupbearer was restored to his job, while the baker was hanged.

Pharaoh's Dreams

PHARAOH'S THRONE
The Pharaoh would have
had a special throne for
religious ceremonies. It
is thought that this
gold-plated throne, found
in Tutankhamen's tomb
in Egypt, was used for
such occasions.

TWO YEARS HAD PASSED and still Joseph was in jail. Then one night Pharaoh had a strange dream: he was standing by the River Nile and while he watched, seven cows, fat and healthy, came out of the water to feed. A little while later seven thin cows came out of the river, so lean and bony they could barely stand.

The thin cows ate up the fat cows. Pharaoh woke with a start. Then he fell asleep and dreamt again. This time he saw seven ears of corn growing plump and golden on a single stalk. Then he saw seven small, shrivelled ears of corn, which devoured the seven large ears.

In the morning Pharaoh demanded that someone be found to explain his dreams. All the wise men and magicians were brought before Pharaoh, but no one could tell him the meaning of his dreams.

Pharaoh

Joseph is brought before Pharaoh and tells him the meaning of his dreams

Joseph

Pharaoh promotes Joseph to the highest office

It was then that the cupbearer remembered Joseph and told Pharaoh how he had correctly interpreted both his and the baker's dreams. Joseph was immediately released from prison and brought before Pharaoh. After thinking for a moment Joseph said, "God has revealed to me what your dreams mean: Egypt is about to enjoy seven years of great plenty, to be followed by seven years of terrible famine. In the time of plenty you must save grain from the harvest and store it, so that there will be enough to eat during the famine."

Pharaoh was so impressed by Joseph that he decided to promote him to the highest office. Pulling the ring from his own finger, he gave it to Joseph, then he hung a heavy gold chain about his neck and dressed him in fine linen robes. He presented him with a magnificent chariot. "You shall be ruler of the whole of Egypt," he declared, "second in power only to myself."

Under Joseph's supervision, grain was gathered and stored during the seven years of good harvest. Then, when the lean years arrived, there was more than enough for all. There was so much that people came from distant lands to buy grain. For the famine was everywhere.

JOSEPH GATHERED CORN AS THE SAND OF THE SEA, VERY MUCH, UNTIL HE LEFT NUMBERING; FOR IT WAS WITHOUT NUMBER.
GENESIS 41:49

CHARIOT
Egyptian chariots were driven by royalty and high officials, as well as by warriors and hunters. When Pharaoh gave a chariot to Joseph, it was a sign of his new status.

Joseph

Under Joseph's supervision, grain is gathered and stored

Life in Egypt

axe   bow   lyre   *women in woollen tunics*   *donkey*   *men in woollen kilts*

WHEN JOSEPH'S FAMILY and friends went to live in Egypt, to escape from famine in their own country, they were given land in Goshen, in the north of the country. This area was part of the Nile Delta, where the River Nile breaks up into many smaller rivers before flowing into the Mediterranean Sea. Because there was plenty of water there, the Israelites were able to grow a great many crops.

An Egyptian schoolboy once described in a letter the comfortable way of life:

FROM CANAAN TO EGYPT
The wall paintings above are from an Egyptian tomb at Beni-Hasan. They show a group of people, probably Canaanites, coming into Egypt with their belongings.

"The countryside provides a wealth of good things. Their pools are full of fish, their lagoons are thick with birds, their meadows are covered with green grass. Their storehouses are full of barley and wheat that tower up to the sky. There are onions and chives to season the food, also pomegranates, apples, olives, and figs from the orchards. People are glad to live there."

ON THE NILE
The River Nile (right) was ancient Egypt's greatest asset. Many vegetables and fruits (left) grew in the fertile land of the Nile valley.

Rulers and Slaves

The rulers of Egypt, the pharaohs, were at the centre of Egyptian society. They lived in great luxury and built rich palaces, temples, and tombs. They were buried inside huge stone pyramids, with their treasures, often made of gold and silver.

Many Israelites became wealthy and some, like Joseph, who had been sold into slavery, rose to have great influence in Egypt. Then, 300 years after Joseph's time, their fortunes changed. In about 1500BC the Egyptian rulers turned against people who had come from other countries: this included the Israelites. They became slaves and had to work for others rather than for themselves.

The Egyptian court was one of the richest of the ancient world.

The Israelites were harshly treated by the Egyptians.

Slaves carried out most of the building work, making bricks from a mixture of mud and straw. Royal buildings were usually made of stone. Israelite slaves may have built the cities of Pithom and Rameses, and the great city of Thebes in the south. The impressive buildings at Thebes and in other parts of Egypt show the skill of builders and craftsmen.

MAP OF THE EXODUS
The route of the Exodus, or exit, from Egypt is not certain. It is likely, however, that the Israelites, led by Moses, avoided the most direct route along the Mediterranean coast so that they did not confront the Philistines in this area.

Moses in Egypt

One of the greatest leaders of the Israelites was Moses, who was found as a baby by the Pharaoh's daughter. He grew up in the grand palaces of the Egyptian court and as a boy would have learnt to read and write in hieroglyphics and take part in popular sports, such as archery and gymnastics.

Moses left Egypt after he had killed an Egyptian. He never forgot that he was an Israelite and he later returned to free his people and lead them out of Egypt at God's command.

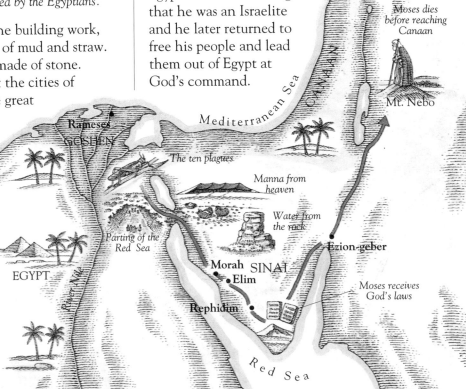

Moses dies before reaching Canaan

Mt. Nebo

CANAAN

Mediterranean Sea

The ten plagues

Manna from heaven

Water from the rock

Parting of the Red Sea

Ezion-geber

EGYPT

River Nile

Morah
Elim
SINAI

Rephidim

Moses receives God's laws

Red Sea

Moses in the Bulrushes

I N EGYPT A NEW PHARAOH came to the throne. Since Joseph's time, the children of Israel had grown powerful and numerous, and the new king was frightened that they would overrun his country. "We must take precautions against them," he said to his counsellors. "If war breaks out, they may side with our enemies and defeat us." First, he gave orders that the Israelites should be treated as slaves, and made to work in gangs building roads and cities. Then he made a ruling that any male child born to an Israelite woman should immediately be put to death.

The Egyptians kill any male child born to an Israelite

Now there was a young married woman of the tribe of Levi who had recently given birth to a boy. Both parents were delighted, and they made up their minds that their son should escape Pharaoh's cruel command.

For the first three months of the baby's life, his mother managed to hide him in the house. But soon he grew too big to hide, and she knew that she could no longer keep him. With a heavy heart, she made a covered cradle out of dried reeds, which she made watertight by covering it with tar and clay. In this she tenderly placed her baby, and left him hidden among the bulrushes on the banks of the Nile.

All this was watched by the baby's sister, who remained near at hand so that she could see what would happen.

It was not long before Pharaoh's daughter, accompanied by her maids, came down to the river to bathe. Catching sight of the little cradle, she sent one of the girls to bring it to her. As the princess gently removed the cover, the baby began to cry, and her heart was touched. "This must be a Hebrew child," she said.

At that moment, the baby's sister came forward and curtseying low to the princess asked if she could be of help.

GOLDEN FISHES
These lucky charms may have been worn to protect against accidents on the River Nile. Made of gold, children probably wore them in their hair.

BASKET
This Egyptian basket and lid dates from 1400BC. Baskets were used as containers for clothes and food in many households. Moses' mother would have found it easy to make one out of papyrus reeds.

"Shall I find a nurse from among the Hebrew women to look after the baby?" she said. The princess was delighted with the suggestion, and the girl ran quickly home to fetch her mother. The princess was happy to employ the woman. "If you will look after the boy," she said, "I will pay you well."

So the baby's real mother was able to bring him up. In time the Pharaoh's daughter, who had grown to love the child, adopted him as her son. "I will call him Moses, which means 'to draw out'," she said, "because I drew him out of the water."

Moses' mother hides her baby among the bulrushes on the banks of the Nile

princess's maids

Moses' sister

KEEPING COOL
Fans made from ostrich feathers were used by servants, known as fan-bearers, in the Egyptian royal court. This ivory-handled fan dates from the time of Moses (c1300BC). Ostriches were a common sight throughout the desert lands of Sinai and Israel in biblical times.

WHEN SHE HAD OPENED IT, SHE SAW THE CHILD: AND, BEHOLD, THE BABE WEPT. AND SHE HAD COMPASSION ON HIM, AND SAID, "THIS IS ONE OF THE HEBREWS' CHILDREN."
EXODUS 2:6

The princess and her servant girl find the baby, as his sister watches from her hiding place

princess

the baby Moses

servant girl

Moses Warns the Pharaoh

Pharaoh

Moses

Aaron

Moses and Aaron stand before Pharaoh and ask him to let their people go, but Pharaoh refuses

AFTER GOD HAD SPOKEN TO HIM, Moses returned home. God had told Moses that the men who wanted to kill him were now dead, and it would be safe for him to go back to Egypt. Moses told his father-in-law of his plan, and asked for his blessing. "Go in peace," said Jethro fondly.

So Moses left Midian, taking with him the staff of God. And accompanied by his wife, his sons, and his brother, Aaron, he came once more to Egypt. He and Aaron went at once to see Pharaoh. "I have come at the command of the God of Israel to ask you to let his people go," said Moses.

Pharaoh smiled coldly. "Why do you stir up trouble among my slaves? I will teach you what it means to defy me!" And he gave orders that the Israelites, who had been put to make bricks out of mud and straw, should no longer have straw provided: they must find it for themselves in the fields.

The Israelites, already worked to exhaustion by their masters, were in despair. "How can we make bricks if we must also gather the straw?" they cried. But their cries were ignored, and those who failed to make as many bricks as before were savagely beaten.

"Look at your people, Lord," said Moses. "They are being treated even more harshly, and there is no hope of release."

SLAVERY
The Egyptians generally treated their slaves well. But the Bible says that as the Israelites grew in number the Egyptians felt threatened. They treated the Israelites harshly, forcing them to build their homes and temples in the hot sun. If they did not work long or hard enough, a supervisor punished them.

The Israelites are beaten by their Egyptian masters

The staffs of Aaron and the royal magicians turn into serpents

Pharaoh

Moses

Aaron

PHARAOH
The powerful rulers of Egypt were called pharaohs. This statue is of Ramesses II, who ruled Egypt during the 13th century BC. It is thought that he was the pharaoh whom Moses spoke to. Ramesses II was responsible for building more monuments and statues than any other pharaoh. Because of these fine achievements, he is often referred to as Ramesses the Great.

"Speak again to Pharaoh," said God. "And demand that he let my people go."

So the brothers stood a second time before Pharaoh and his court, only to receive the same answer. But Moses, remembering what God had told him, signalled to Aaron to throw down the staff. Aaron did so, and as the staff touched the ground it turned into a serpent. At this Pharaoh gave the order to his royal magicians, and they all threw down their staffs which all turned into serpents. These were swallowed up by Aaron's serpent.

But Pharaoh remained unmoved.

"Go to the banks of the Nile," said the Lord to Moses. "And when Pharaoh comes down to the river, ask him again to let my people go. And if he will not, strike the surface of the water with your staff."

And so Moses and Aaron went down to the river, and waited for Pharaoh to come.

SERPENT
One of the gods worshipped by the Egyptians was the serpent god, Sito, shown above. When Aaron's serpent ate the Egyptian serpents, it showed God's power over the Egyptian gods.

The Plagues of Egypt

ONCE MORE, Moses and Aaron pleaded with Pharaoh to let the people go. When Pharaoh refused to listen, they struck the waters of the River Nile. At once the water turned to blood, and all the fish died, and the dead fish rotted in the sun and stank. For seven days the whole of Egypt ran with blood, and there was no water to drink. But Pharaoh refused to free the Israelites. So Moses and Aaron, following God's command, stretched their sacred staff over the Nile. At once, throughout all Egypt, frogs in their hundreds and thousands came hopping out of rivers, streams and ponds, hopping into people's houses, into their cupboards and ovens, even into their beds.

The waters of the Nile turn to blood and all the fish die

Horrified, Pharaoh sent for Moses. "Ask your god to take away this plague," he implored. "And I will let your people go at once!" Overnight the frogs died. They lay several deep in the villages and fields, until they were gathered up into evil-smelling heaps.

Frogs hop into people's houses

And when Pharaoh saw that the plague of frogs was over, he went back on his word.

Then Aaron took his staff and struck the sand beneath his feet, and the millions of grains of sand turned into millions of lice, which crawled and seethed over every man, woman and beast in the land.

Lice crawl over every man and woman

But Pharaoh's heart was like stone.

Next came a cloud of flies, fat, black flies which crawled into people's mouths and under their eyelids.

Again Pharaoh begged Moses, in return for the Israelites' freedom, to rid him of the plague. And when the flies were gone, again he broke his word.

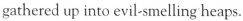

A cloud of flies attack the people

All the oxen are struck by disease

This time the Lord sent disease to Egypt, which killed every horse and camel, all the oxen, the goats and the sheep, every one.

But still Pharaoh would not let the children of Israel leave.

God said to Moses and Aaron, "Take a handful of ashes from the fire and throw it up into the air." And as they did this, the ashes spread a hideous sickness which broke out in boils, covering the skin of both men and animals.

People are covered in boils

But Pharaoh was not moved.

Then God told Moses to stretch his hand towards the heavens, and instantly there was a crash of thunder, red-hot lightning zigzagged along the ground, and a heavy hail fell from the sky, flattening whole fields and smashing open the trunks of trees.

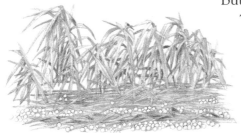

Heavy hail flattens whole fields

Pharaoh summoned Moses. "Now I will do as you ask if you will stop the storm." So Moses spoke to the Lord, and the hail and thunder stopped. But the children of Israel were not released.

That same day an east wind began to blow; it blew all day and all night, and with the wind came the locusts. They came in such numbers that the sky was black, and they covered the land so that the land was black, and they ate every remaining blade of grass, every leaf, every fruit left hanging from the tree.

When Pharaoh repented, God turned the wind, and the locusts were blown into the Red Sea. But his people were kept captive still.

Locusts cover the sky and fields

So God told Moses to stretch out his hand, and darkness fell upon Egypt, and there was no light for three days.

Pharaoh sent for Moses. "Now you may go, you and all your people, but you must leave your flocks behind."

"That I may not do," said Moses.

"Then I shall keep your people as slaves, and I forbid you ever to come into my presence again. If you disobey me in this, you will die."

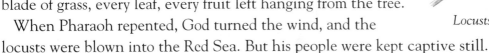

Darkness falls for three days

The Tenth Plague

*The Israelites daub the doorposts
of their houses with blood*

*In every Egyptian family, the
eldest child dies*

PASSOVER FEAST
Today, Jewish people celebrate Passover once a year. The various foods symbolize the Exodus: unleavened bread, a nut and apple paste called charoseth, horseradish and lettuce (the bitter herbs), a roasted lamb-bone, eggs, and salt water.

THE LORD SPOKE TO MOSES. "I shall bring one last plague to Egypt, a plague so terrible that Pharaoh will have no choice but to let my people go. At midnight tonight every first-born child throughout the country will die. Not one shall escape: all will die, from the first born of Pharaoh himself, to the first born of the poorest slave, to the first born of the cattle in the fields. Only the children of Israel will remain untouched.

"This day shall for ever afterwards be known as Passover, for tonight I will pass over the whole of Egypt, and my people will be freed. From now on, the day must be kept holy and counted as the first day of the year. Every household must kill a lamb, which shall then be roasted and eaten with bitter herbs and bread that is unleavened. Your doorposts must be daubed with the blood of the slain animal, so that when I pass in the night I shall know to leave untouched the houses marked with blood."

Moses called together all his wise men and counsellors and told them what God had said, and how they were to keep this day, the first Passover, holy for ever after.

Midnight fell, and suddenly a terrible wailing and screaming was heard, the Lord passed over the land. Except for the Israelites, not one family was left unharmed. Death was everywhere. Everywhere, from

AND PHARAOH CALLED FOR MOSES AND AARON BY NIGHT, AND SAID, "RISE UP AND GET YOU FORTH FROM AMONG MY PEOPLE, BOTH YE AND THE CHILDREN OF ISRAEL; AND GO, SERVE THE LORD, AS YE HAVE SAID."
EXODUS 12:31

Taking all their possessions with them, the Israelites leave Egypt

Pharaoh's palace to the darkest prison, from the rich merchant's house to the open pasture, the first born, both man and beast, drew its last breath and died.

Pharaoh, rising from his bed in grief, sent for Moses and Aaron. "Take your people and go! Go from my country, and take all your flocks and herds!" By now, the Egyptians were so frightened they begged the Israelites to leave as quickly as possible, and heaped their former slaves with silver, gold and jewels.

And so it was that after four hundred and thirty years of captivity the children of Israel, six hundred thousand of them, all on foot, men, women and children, with their flocks and herds and all their possessions, at last left Egypt.

SADDLE-BAG
On leaving Egypt, the Israelites may have carried their possessions in saddle-bags, similar to this Bedouin one made of goat's hair and wool.

The Crossing of the Red Sea

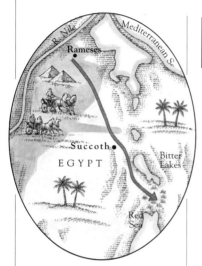

CROSSING THE SEA
The Hebrew words originally translated as "Red Sea" in fact mean "sea of reeds". It is possible that the Israelites crossed over a marshy swamp to the north of the Red Sea.

THE RED SEA
The Israelites could have camped at a spot like this by the Red Sea. The sea usually looks blue, but when the algae that grow in the water die, the sea becomes a reddish-brown.

GOD LED HIS PEOPLE OUT OF EGYPT and through the wilderness at the edge of the Red Sea. He led them by day as a column of cloud and by night as a column of fire, so they should know which way to go.

But Pharaoh again hardened his heart, angry that he had let his slaves leave. He gave orders to the officers of his army to make ready, and himself led a force of six hundred chariots, as well as horsemen and foot soldiers, against the Israelites.

The Israelites were camped on the shore when they saw the Egyptian army approaching. They turned in terror to Moses. "Why did you take us from our comfortable captivity only to let us die here in the wilderness?"

"Do not be afraid," Moses reassured them. "The Lord will protect you from harm."

As he spoke, the column of cloud moved over the Egyptians, so that they were in darkness. Then, following the word of the Lord, Moses stretched his hand over the sea. Immediately a strong wind sprang up, and the waters parted, and a passage of dry land appeared along the sea-bed. Moses led his people along this path, the waters like a high wall on either side of them.

As soon as Pharaoh saw what was happening, he and his army came galloping in pursuit. But as his horsemen and his hundreds of chariots thundered over the dry sand, the Lord commanded Moses again to stretch out his hand. The waters of the Red Sea closed over the Egyptians, and every man was drowned.

But the children of Israel reached the far side in safety, and when they saw how God had protected them, they gave grateful thanks to him and to his prophet, Moses.

Then Miriam, the sister of Moses and Aaron, took up her tambourine, and calling the other women to follow her, led them in a dance along the water's edge. As they danced they sang a song of praise, recalling the happy escape of the children of Israel from their long years of slavery, and their crossing of the Red Sea.

The waters of the Red Sea close
over the Egyptians

AND THE CHILDREN OF ISRAEL
WENT INTO THE MIDST OF THE
SEA UPON THE DRY GROUND.
EXODUS 14:22

Miriam takes a
tambourine and dances
with the other women

Moses and his people cross on dry land and
reach the far side in safety

God Watches Over the Israelites

Flocks of quail appear in the desert

The Israelites catch the quails and roast them

QUAILS
Migrating quails fly across the Sinai Desert twice a year. Tired from the long flight, they fly low and are easily caught.

MANNA
Some scholars think that the manna may have come from the hammada shrub, above, which grows in southern Sinai. When insects feed on its branches, it produces a sweet, white liquid. Today, Bedouin people use it as a sweetener.

THE ISRAELITES WANDERED in the Sinai Desert for many weeks, hungry and exhausted. They began to whisper against Moses and Aaron. "At least in Egypt we had plenty to eat, but here we may die of starvation."

The Lord heard what they were saying, and told Moses to summon his people. "They shall be well provided with food," God promised.

In the morning the ground is covered with manna from heaven

The people are told to gather as much as they can eat in a day

That same evening there suddenly appeared flocks of quail, which were caught and roasted.

The next morning the ground was covered with small round shapes, white and tasting of honey. The Israelites were puzzled. "What is this?" they asked each other. "It must be manna, for it falls from Heaven."

"This is bread sent by God," said Moses. "Let the people gather as much as they can eat in a day, and no more." But some were greedy and took more than their share. Secretly they hoarded the manna in their tents, and overnight it turned black, and became full of worms and stank.

On the sixth day, Moses told them they could collect enough food to last for two days. "Tomorrow is a holy day of rest, as decreed by God. Today you must gather up what you need, and eat as much as you want and keep the rest for the Sabbath. It will stay fresh and good overnight, for tomorrow you will find no manna on the ground."

Most people did as Moses said, but a few disobeyed and went out on the Sabbath looking for food.

"When will the people learn to obey my rules?" the Lord asked Moses.

The days passed and the Israelites, as they made their slow way through the burning desert, complained of a lack of water. "Why did you bring us out of Egypt just to die of thirst?" they asked angrily.

But God told Moses to go to a certain rock and strike it with his staff. As he did so, water cold and pure gushed out of the rock, so that they all could drink their fill.

As Moses strikes the rock with his staff, water gushes out

"BEHOLD, I WILL STAND BEFORE THEE THERE UPON THE ROCK IN HOREB; AND THOU SHALT SMITE THE ROCK, AND THERE SHALL COME WATER OUT OF IT, THAT THE PEOPLE MAY DRINK." AND MOSES DID SO IN THE SIGHT OF THE ELDERS OF ISRAEL.
EXODUS 17:6

Moses Receives God's Laws

AND MOSES DREW NEAR UNTO
THE THICK DARKNESS WHERE
GOD WAS.
EXODUS 20:21

AFTER THREE MONTHS the children of Israel arrived at the foot of the holy mountain of Sinai, where they made their camp. Moses went up the mountain to pray to God, who told him that in three days he himself would speak to the people.

On the morning of the third day the sky turned black, and thunder and lightning crashed and rumbled through the darkness. The mountain itself belched smoke and fire like a great furnace, and the ground shook. Then the voice of God was heard like a mighty trumpet, calling Moses to him.

God calls Moses to him and gives him the ten commandments carved on two stone tablets

"I am the Lord your God, and these are my commandments, to be obeyed by all my people.

You shall worship no other God but me.

You shall not make any statue or picture to worship.

You shall not speak the name of the Lord except with reverence.

You shall keep the sabbath, the seventh day, as a holy day of rest, for in six days I made the world, but on the seventh day I rested.

You shall show respect to your father and mother.

You shall not commit murder.

You shall not be unfaithful to your husband or wife.

You shall not steal.

You shall not speak falsely against others.

You shall not envy another person's possessions."

When the people heard the thunder and saw the flames and the smoke, they were terrified and would not come near. But Moses reassured them. "Do not be afraid," he said. "God has come to us so that we may learn his commandments and keep ourselves free of sin."

But still the people shrank back, and again Moses went up the mountain alone, to the dark cloud on the summit where God was.

MOUNT SINAI
Moses received God's laws on Mount Sinai, or Mount Horeb, as it is sometimes called in the Bible. Mount Sinai is believed to be the mountain Jebel Musa or "Mountain of Moses", part of a group of peaks in the south of the Sinai peninsula. It is 2,300 m (7,500 ft) high and is made of red granite.

The Israelites camp at the foot of the holy mountain of Sinai

Index

Who's Who in the Bible Stories

AARON Moses' brother, who was his spokesman when they met Pharaoh. *Pages 49, 50-51, 52*

ABRAHAM/ABRAM The first Patriarch of the Israelites. His faith in God made him a great leader. *Pages 18-29*

ADAM The first man. *Pages 10-11, 12*

ESAU Jacob's twin brother and the son of Isaac and Rebekah. *Pages 30-32, 36-37*

EVE The first woman. *Pages 10-11*

HAGAR The servant of Sarah and the mother of Ishmael. *Pages 20-21*

HAM One of Noah's three sons. *Page 12*

ISAAC Son of Abraham and Sarah and the father of Jacob and Esau. *Pages 21, 26-32*

ISHMAEL Son of Abraham and Hagar, Sarah's servant. *Page 21*

ISRAEL The name later given to Jacob and his descendants. *Page 37*

JACOB One of Isaac's sons who stole Esau's inheritance. Father of the 12 tribes of Israel *Pages 30-37, 38*

JAPHETH One of Noah's three sons. *Page 12*

JETHRO Moses' father-in-law. *Pages 48, 50*

JOSEPH Jacob's favourite son. He was sold into slavery in Egypt, then rose to a position of power. *Pages 38-43*

JUDAH One of Jacob's 12 sons. *Page 39*

LABAN Rebekah's brother. Father of Rachel and Leah. *Pages 29, 32, 35, 36*

LEAH Daughter of Laban and Jacob's wife. *Page 35*

LOT Abraham's nephew who lived in Sodom. *Pages 18-19, 23-25*

MOSES The man who led the Israelites out of Egypt to search for the promised land. *Pages 6-7, 45-61*

NOAH He and his family were saved from death in the great flood by building a boat. *Pages 12-15*

POTIPHAR The Egyptian courtier for whom Joseph worked. *Pages 40-41*

RACHEL Jacob's favourite wife. The mother of Joseph and Benjamin. *Pages 34-35, 38*

REBEKAH Isaac's wife, the mother of Jacob and Esau. *Pages 28-32*

REUBEN Jacob's eldest son. *Page 39*

SARAH/SARAI Abraham's wife and the mother of Isaac. *Pages 18-22*

SATAN The name sometimes given to the Devil, who is thought to be the source of all sin and evil. *Page 10*

Acknowledgements

Photographic Credits
l=left, r=right, t=top, c=centre, b=bottom

Ancient Art & Architecture Collection: 42tl.
Ardea:/ Wardene Weisser: 58tl.
Barnaby's Picture Library: 36bl.
BBC Radio Vision: 6br, 7tl.
Bridgeman Art Library: 6tl.
Trustees of the British Museum: 7c, 10bl, 18tl, 18tr, 19t, 46tl, 46bl, 47tr, 51br.
Professor A. Danin, Jerusalem: 58cl.
Mary Evans Picture Library: 14tl.
Giraudon: 41br.
Sonia Halliday: 27tr, 56bl, 61tr.
Hamburger Kunsthalle: 35t.
Robert Harding Picture Library: 17tr, 34b, 41tr, 43cr, 50cl, 54bl.

Michael Holford: 40bl, 51tr.
Hutchinson Picture Library: 7b, 19br, 20tl, 21tr, 35b.
Israel Museum, Jerusalem: 7tr The Shrine of the Book.
Kunsthistorisches Vienna © Mayer: 44t.
NHPA:/Anthony Bannister 10tl.
Oxford Scientific Films: 29tr.
Planet Earth:/ Peter Stephenson 30tl.
Dino Politis: 13br, 17br.
Zev Radovan: 12tl, 15tr, 25br.
Sheila Weir: 29br.
Zefa: 26tl, 26bl, 28bl, 44bc.

Dorling Kindersley would like to thank:
Tim Ridley, Nick Goodall and Gary Ombler at the DK Studio; Dorian Spencer Davies; Antonio Forcione; Christopher Gillingwater; Polly Goodman; George Hart; Alan Hills; James W. Hunter; Robin Hunter; Marcus James; Anna Kunst; Michelle de Larrabeiti; Antonio Montoro; Anderley Moore; Jackie Ogburn; Derek Peach; Lenore Person; Dino Politis; Lara Tankel Holtz and Martin Wilson for their help in producing this book.

Picture research by: Diana Morris

Index by: Lynn Bresler